Love Inn!

Timothée Bordenave

Ukiyoto Publishing

All global publishing rights are held by
Ukiyoto Publishing
Published in 2025

Content Copyright © Timothée Bordenave
ISBN 9789370096455
*All rights reserved.
No part of this publication may be reproduced,
transmitted, or stored in a retrieval system, in any
form by any means, electronic, mechanical,
photocopying, recording or otherwise, without the
prior permission of the publisher.*

The moral rights of the author have been asserted.

*This book is sold subject to the condition that it shall
not by way of trade or otherwise, be lent, resold, hired
out or otherwise circulated, without the publisher's
prior consent, in any form of binding or cover other
than that in which it is published.*

www.ukiyoto.com

Dedication

This book is dedicated to the French people, and to my country, France. With all my loving heart... Might our Lord keep us all ! Timothée.

Contents

Unicorns records	1
In the dark	2
Enchantress	3
Christian poem	4
Devoted	5
I hid a treasure !	6
A simple life	7
Deer king	8
La Madeleine	9
Misty morning	10
Be simple	11
The party	12
In Berlin	12
he Elephant	13
Wild Encounters	14
Upper Class	15
-Self Irony-	15
Casual Millionaire	16
Treasure in the Sky	17
The lights	18
Love letter to a friend	19
Inner Temple, London	20
London by Night	21
London, you can !	23
A Little Greenery	24

Hush now, pretty French boy…	25
United they stand…	26
One for all !	27
Union of prayers	28
Giving graces…	29
Emy - Angel	30
Benedictions	31
My secrets	32
A new life !	33
Do you know Parmenides ?	34
The Law.	35
Rhyme	35
Curriculum Vitae of the poet…	36
Dedication	37
Goodbye for now !	38
About the Author	*40*

Unicorns records

It is said unicorns live beneath apple trees,
In orchards, on the misty South West Cornwall shores,
I heard, then it is a statement from our Lore,
They are intelligent, mighty, brave, proud and free.

A mage once taught me, deep in Brittany forests,
« The unicorns can fly, to assist, everywhere,
A person who would be facing threat or despair…
And, they also appear sometimes, to those who quest. »

He followed : « If by chance, you see one, just keep calm,
Those creatures are magic itself, in many senses,
They choose you to reveal their mystical presence. »

I read in an old book : this happens to the child,
The virgin, and the wise, and some knights, in the wild…
In Paris a tapestry shows them, dearing a « Dame ».

In the dark

Have you ever been all alone,
In a wood at night, with no lamp,
Off the tracks, thirsty, with a cramp,
Chased after in an army zone ?

Few have. I heard, once, close to Death,
The hits of bullets, missing me !
Yet as I ran, the enemy -
Forces, left my surroundings. Safe.

It was passed midnight, far from mines,
I came across a trail that lead,
Luckily, soon, to a village,

Where I hid. There's no privilege,
When war takes you : quickly I fled,
To hide again, in an old mine.

Enchantress

O beautiful you I adore,
Lady of Glamour, Queen of Charms,
When will you sleep deep in my arms,
Again, whilst suns rise on the shore ?

O fayrie ! Tender, true princess,
Our love has caught and casts the last -
Bloom for spring, heart beats like a blast,
They will not cease, never know less…

Yes ! But now for you are away,
I am lonely in Paris,
My soul prays sole until the day.

I remember these times of ore,
Plenty of laughter, full of bliss,
Might our Lord join us soon, for more !

Christian poem

O Lord, Thy above all the clouds,
All the sky, the Sun and the stars,
Please save me Timothee, I hold,
This prayer to my life. I stare…

Life is your gift, blessed from the air,
I hear your voice in my heart, loud !
Thy inner, around or afar,
My animal songs, to Thy howled…

I want to express gratitude,
Please keep me in your Paradise,
Where the Angels rule to all eyes !

Let me have a good attitude !
Please Lord, forgive me if I missed.
For Jesus' love. Forever his !

Devoted

If I act with benevolence,
Humility, manners, and calm,
If in my heart I sing the psalms,
Of Heaven, then I write my stances !

Well o Lord thy might grant me grace,
Through the Love that comes from the Skies,
I shall live ! Under your embrace,
We are meek children, you are wise.

The beauty of the World has seized,
My existence in a prayer,
Then praying helped me, praying eased…

The darkness I may have known prior,
It vanished ! No my days are pleased,
When in devotion, I admire.

I hid a treasure !

I hid an important treasure,
At a mansion, in South West France,
In the middle of this immense,
Park - where I often took leisure.

The diamonds or the rubies,
The gold, the gems, the jewelry…
Are kept there - until memory,
Would cess maybe - there they will be.

Am I a fool, led by romance,
Out of my reason for hence,
Leaving in Nature, a fortune ?

Well - forever would be immune,
My life in Heaven if I'm worth…
That's my only burden, my oath.

A simple life

I live here, Avenue of Sister Rosalie,
Who was a generous, charitable person.
Full of kindness, of grace… - She gives inspiration,
To me, painter and poet, I pray her humbly.

Close from me, there's a park, where I go walk the lanes,
And the birds sing aloud in the bushes of flowers…
I love this place, some kids go by, I rest an hour,
Then I get back to my readings - where I pertain.

Then, that's it ! And I reach outside for groceries,
Tobacco, brew, rarely to a social event,
But I am solitary, I work, or I chant…

Inner, the bright motives of my love for Jesus,
To the Angels I see around, secrets, for us,
Only - This is my life ! Simple life in Paris.

Deer king

There is an old saying by some ancient French woods,
That a deer might be Lord, of all of the forests…
A white deer ! With a ruby cross seen at his chest,
And four lions flank him, companions, or knighthood.

It is a known legend ! It might as well be true,
As the mages, the druids, the bards, often tell.
They say the deer comes with a charm none could repel,
Of life, or death, eternal, according to you.

If I can remember once I saw the white king,
On my path, I was lost and striving for water.
He disappeared, I collapsed, then fell, but after…

After yes, I rose up, then found a stream to drink.
I am not sure ! If I can recall well, I think :
Soon, I found a shelter, guided by dogs barking.

La Madeleine

We were climbing, once in Paris,
On the roof of La Madeleine,
Famous church, close to river Seine.
Suddenly I felt all blurry…

« You will die, fool ! » Cried the traitor.
« I drugged you… » - He tried to push me.
I bent over a scale. « Implore,
Your God ! » Shouted my enemy.

Luckily after a quick fight,
I kicked him enough, he fainted…
Around us was a cloudy night.

I was in a fuzz and in stress,
Sat here for a while, I rested,
Climbed down and left !
              - Oh, my Lord bless !

Misty morning

It is a little farm, in the wild, up a hill,

There has been snow this night : white cover on the fields,

I wake up in the misty dawn when just revealed,

The Sun, everything is quiet and is still.

« Well, brother Sun, you might be shining all your lights,

Then you could maybe heat us down here a little ! »

Think-I. And I walk down the snows, pass the stable,

Reach the kitchen, pour coffee. Morning will be bright !

I hear the dogs grunting, as they enter the room.

I greet them. They get out… « Lord knows what dreams a dog ! »

Alone again, I start a new stove with two logs.

While thinking : « Our lives are full of an unknown,

Yet perceivable fact, there is more to be shown,

Around… » I sit and eat, toasts with jelly of plum.

Be simple

The most humble is happiest.
The most efficient, most simple.
Good hearts beat in many people…
Common sense knows how to harvest !

And there is far more, there is Love !
There are birds, singing by the grove,
Nature all around, abundance,
Mystery ! As the children dance…

We are blessed ! Oh, I knew sorrows,
In times past yes, but still I hope,
For better days and tomorrows…

Yes, the Skies hold us on their scope,
We men, women, youngsters, should know,
Joy, desire, waters of hop.

The party
In Berlin

There was music around, all of us were dancing,

To the loud, frenetic melody and scansion,

Though we were three hundred, we would not feel tension,

Only the love, the smiles, as these speakers would sing…

Yes ! Even if I had come alone to the place,

I was feeling upheld by the crowd as I moved,

With the rhythm, so strong ! Soon our party improved :

When I saw at my side a cute girl's smiling face.

« Mm » Thought-I. « This woman is pretty ! Attractive ! »

And I bounced for some more, my eyes shut, with a smile…

Then there after we kissed. I proposed we would leave.

We walked for a moment in the surrounding woods,

Let apart what followed when a quarter of mile,

Further, we sat and leaned, and kissed, and kissed, moulded…

The Elephant

I saw a bathing elephant,
In a pond, once in Cambodia,
Very tall, massive, elegant,
He splashed along with euphoria…

« Sire ! » Addressed-I to the beast,
« Oh, what a joy to me also,
To see you happy, makes me so,
Glad, inner ! I feel my heartbeats… »

He replied in a loud trumpet,
Some words I didn't understand,
In Khmer… Then rolled up on the sands.

« Cheers to you, graces to the Skies !
Glories to Ganesha the wise…
I witnessed here their true prophet. »

Wild Encounters

I saw a lynx, the lynx cut links,
He disappeared behind a sage…
I saw a red collar, mirage !
The bird flew elsewhere in a blink…

I saw a deer, I said « My dear,
Stay for more ! » But he jumped afar…
I saw three gooses and a jar,
They winged further off - maybe near…

And then I saw a crocodile,
Resting in the waters of Nile,
He yawned, he slowly clasped his mouth…

Then approached, with a little trot,
But with all reverence to Thot,
I soon ran away. Far enough !

Upper Class
-Self Irony-

Now, you see me as someone new !
There has been a shift in my thoughts,
Yes, because yesterday I bought,
A new flat, on the avenue…

Oh ! I am no more a rebel,
I am not a modest author,
Anymore, I might be later,
A star, of poems and novels…

No, do not offer me cheap wine
I will drink Burgundy, with taste,
At my chic parties, say : my feists !

No, no more of stained white sneakers,
I wear chic, daim derbies, kickers,
Off your bottom, you vagrant, vain !

Casual Millionaire

When I used to be a hippie,
Smoking my cigarettes of herb,
Walking around in the suburb,
To be true, I was not happy.

I was lacking acknowledgement.
This is not a joke ! I felt free,
Maybe but I was in torment,
Mislead, vague, close to misery…

Today I am a millionaire.
I worked hard, published twenty books,
And painted a lot. If I look…

Back again to the days I erred,
I miss you now, gentle lovers,
By my side !
        Counting on flowers…

Treasure in the Sky

Yes ! I have silks, and branded clothes,
I have the carpets, the gemstones,
The gold, rare shells of abalones,
Rare masks, and coins, my house encloses,

Yes ! I have buried five treasures,
Upon my countryside estates,
Then now I collect for leisure,
Diamonds or old wines of taste…

Though it is only for thy Lord,
That I want to live furthermore,
Please hear me, o Skies I adore…

Lead me on a meriting path,
Keep me praying, until I pass,
Then I hope, a new life accord !

The lights

I used to be, and still am I
Devotee to the mystical,
Nature, Faith, Love of the Most High,
Who is said our Lord biblical.

Would you believe me when I state,
I read twenty thousand pages,
Of philosophy and the mages,
Then I sat down, to contemplate ?

This I did. And I wrote a book,
Trying to express gratitude,
While I rested, in solitude…

And now, well, as far as I look,
Inner, outer, further, before…
All I can see are lights of ore.

Love letter to a friend

By these banks of the Thames river, when tide is low...
There's a strand of wet sands, dirty and abandoned,
To the nostalgia of dreamers in London,
For anyone could walk there... Often I did so.

By a misty - foggy I would say - dawning hour,
Once I left a letter to you, Bobbie, my dear !
On a clutch. In a pouch. By the bank. As you near,
The point of view where you admire our great Tower.

Please, go pick my letter, in a crack in cement !
It has been here for years, waiting for you old friend...
When you climb at the scale, just above a garment.

Who knows ? Unless I do ! There are told our secrets...
When sun rises, a beam on metal, lets you find,
Our love letter - prudence, cherished ! Be delicate.

Inner Temple, London

There's an hidden lane yard in London, BlackFriars,
Where are the Courts of Law, pleasant, of reds and greys...
As you reach the East exit, from Inner Templar,
You will see a basin, where I sat and I prayed...

Oh ! Lord ! I was saddened by these days in London...
When I was just a child, feeling sorrow and pain,
But when I walked this path to school, the horizon,
Of my thoughts, by magic, would clear, at this fountain.

London, Inner Temple courtyard, I remember !
An Angel came to me, once there I was crying.
She told me I would need to be strong, then yonder...

Further, my life would heal, I shall be happier.
I came back to France ! Healed...
                      And there are still lying,
The diamonds I left to you, Angel, lawyer !

London by Night

To a young foreigner…

Did you ever walk by London, at night, alone ?
Just walk, just contemplate the city, its magic !
You could wander forever, maybe, nostalgic.
Admire : the streets, the clouds, the jewels of the Crown…

They are all there before your feet, it's infinite,
In that sense you could not, I believe, in your life,
See all of these, for sure… Be it haven, or strife,
Be it loom or a joy, a grey dusk, dark, or light…

Follow this way : you reach, out of Tate Modern,
By the waters, Southwark, the Globe, then Tower Bridge.
Cross to Saint Kathrine Docks, stay a while on a bench…

Walk backwards, reach Saint Paul, there's a pub where to quench,
Meet an old mariner there, tell him you are lige,

To the blessed Kings of France !
Pay him, leave this tavern…

London, you can !

London, London by night, London at dusk, at dawn…
You would be forever in my heart with the psalms.
I heard your chants, Christians, with their Anglican charms,
In a church where I wept. Whilst Christmas had just shown…

You, English women and men, know the tales of Lore,
The ballads and the rhymes, and legends from old times.
I do believe in them, in their power, their prime !
I believe in the might from the mist at your shores…

London ! England ! You can make a young boy, a man.
Yes, I was on a thrive and sorrowful and lost,
Then I prayed ! I recall many nights if not most :

When I was in my room, puzzled, bent for mercy…
Thy o Lord delivered your child, for now I see,
Banks of Thames, twenty years later,
                    By Easter's shine.

A Little Greenery

When I was a young folk, at Elephant and Castle,
I met no elephant, no snake, beast, nor cattle,
I saw no fortress, nor a manor, no palace,
But I used to go down a pub, to drink a glass…

This pub was « The Green Elf » where Jamaicans drove,
A little enterprise, entertainment I prized !
There I would get easily, for a decent price,
Some of these small sachets, with clouds inside, of love…

It is so beautiful that this world, we live in,
Lets the seeds travel far, and their gardeners too !

You would find a secret life, only few have seen,
In London City yes, my dear, if you search well…

The Kings at Buckingham slept while I slipped into :
The clouds… Elvens and fays, liquors, through my heart dwelled.

Hush now, pretty French boy...

"Oh hip hip hip hooray, for Tim !" Chanted them all,
At the university, we were having lunch,
Joyful fellows, we were drinking, a beer, a punch,
It was about my eighteenth birthday... End of fall.

We were sat at the Peacock Pub, close from the Strand,
Where is the London School for the Economy !
They were partying there, happily, this for me !
Timothee the Second, Duke of Blue Magic Wands.

But I was desperate. At my sides two young girls,
Students like me, would cheer, even kiss on my cheeks...
I was a fortunate, glamorous, clever, "chic"...

And sad, pretty French boy, in England studying law...

Well, to my friends Angels, who I love, who I owe,
Thanks ! Joy has won... Praises still drift, to your robe curled.

United they stand…

There is something hidden in United Kingdom,

Would you spend some time there, you would guess, I believe,

Of how can these people assume the way they live ?

Half Lords and Peers, half punks, half bourgeois, scholars some…

An oddity appears in their History bookshelves :

They invaded every countries in our whole world,

Except Lesotho, then quickly came back to fold,

Their sails, and drink whisky, sleep tight, all by themselves…

There is more : it is a known fact, I have seen it,

When young folks in London, go for a party out,

They are all half naked, in the cold, with no coat,

They would explain : "We don't want to pay a locker…"

Whilst, I don't know how they could avoid the doctor ?

Mystery rule these lands. With magic, and some wit.

One for all !

O Saint Lord, blessed of all, and of far more than all,
Thy are not bound inner the walls of Vatican,
We know Thy Orthodox, Lutheran, Anglican,
Calvinist, Maroonist, Greek, Copt… Christ has the whole…

Better yet : the Hebrews were first to pray Thy name,
Believers of Islam, love Thee since ancient times…
Long did Buddha pray Thee, prophet without a grime,
Then to all of Hindus, your Legend is the Fame !

Nô, to the Japanese, Great Spirit to Bantus,
Ineffable Tao in China, Wakan Tan…
Thy are one for us all, all in one, for Thy can !

Then I believe Mages, counting their arcanas,
A Voodoo, a Wizard, or Witch, or Shamana…
All are yours, as the fays, and the unicorns too !

Union of prayers

Unicorns of this World, unite !
And get along with us, poets,
Then our alliance, infinite,
Shall rule this lovely planet…

O Fays, o Mages, come around !
We shall dance in a sarabande,
Until we find some common grounds,
With all prophets, from all far lands…

Morning, day, to dusk, night, till dawn,
Brother Sun, keeper of our dreams,
Sister Moon, grace on your soft beams…

Join us ! We know the Angels own,
Everything for Christ… Wonders,
Join Us ! Pixies, Salamanders…

Giving graces…

Here, I wanted to say : thank you,
From the very depth of my heart,
For all of this beautiful art,
For every books I went through…

For all of your joyful ideas,
Each of your gifts, each of the flowers !
Thanks for the laughter, for these hours,
Of love, of joy, of peace, of ease.

I am a simple man ! I eat,
I drink, I work, and rest some time,
Interact with people I meet…

Lucky to walk by on my feet !
You are my treasure from a dime,
Thanks, o Jesus ! I wish I'll fit…

Emy - Angel

« You know well how I love you dear ! »

« I love you too so very much… »

« When we lay, as morning comes near,
I cherish your embrace, your touch !

Then when you wake up in a smile,
I look at you pouring some tea,
Half naked… Angel from the Isles,
You are beautiful ! »

    « Timothy !
You already told this to me !
I am not an Angel at all…
I am a simple girl ! »

    « Emy !
I am writing at the moment,
A poem to express my whole,
Adoration, o firmament… »

Benedictions

Thy o Lord in the Skies, above,
Know of how much I revere,
In my heart your wise, tender love,
Mysteries, Thy will forever.

Oh the beautiful shade or light,
Oh praises given, blessings brought,
Through a humble life, long were sought,
Destiny's chances, Thy all might !

When bent over my work table,
I worship the benedictions,
Of life itself, praying for peace…

Thy o Lord saint, please enable,
Better thoughts and better actions,
While I hope from Heavens a piece…

My secrets

Once to a phlegmatic, British girl in Paris,
I taught all my secrets : « Prayer is alchemy,
Love is light, peace is safe, ignore the enemy,
You would never be too hurt if your mind is free…

Be mobile, be tender, be liquid as water,
And positively try just to act with good will,
There after you could not fear any encounter,
Yet, if someone fights you… Fight ! Otherwise keep still.

When the Angels above want to gift us with grace,
They are unseen, but soon their blessings will reveal,
Knee then, or bow before their soft, happy embrace…

Oh ! And work ! From your work would your life be success ! »

This girl, named Sue, listened to me then she appealed,
My lips to hers,
        She smiled, and silently we kissed.

A new life !

It's often two warm hearts find a new home in love…
A mystical silence soon follows, intertwined,
With a scansion of sounds, well, as their passion wins,
Kisses and joyful plays melt bodies instinct drove…

Then it also happens often : a child is born,
Then an other, later, a few, eventually…
This is what we humans call a true family,
Elders, lovers, and kids, for Nature to adorn.

One fine day all gather, to a brunch in a park,
By a sunny morning, in the shade of an oak,
To spend some good moments, with their friends, or cousins…

And at the magical instants when sings a lark,
It is said, I heard it, two grown up cute young folks,
Find love again ! O Virtue ! A new life begins…

(Thanks to my dear Anna !)

Do you know Parmenides ?

There is a mystical, whimsy, magical wit,
In the ancient scriptures of all philosophers,
That resides in the fact that after many hours,
When reading such a book, no one understands it.

Let me be clear : you could work on Parmenides,
For one year long, and truly enjoy doing so,
Then you could not think I, explain any ideas,
Of such an Ancient thought, mysterious « in ipso ! »

Perhaps because at first, you would need all your life,
In a patient study, to compare with their peers,
Parmenides, Thales, Plato, Aristotle…

Perhaps. Then I would say : it's almost a defy,
To me, to cook a pie, or a jelly of pears…
Thus how could I pretend that « I know Sophocles » ?

The Law.
Rhyme

« Love each other, as yourself,
And love our Lord, most of all…
Then you will have lived the whole,
Of the Law. » Said the Queen Elf.

She was quoting Jesus Christ,
Saint of all saints, son of God,
Light from the light, realm, abode,
First before firsts, last, till lasts…

« Majesty, was it allowed,
When Evan took my honey,
To eat it ? » Asked Peleg, imp…

« Evan shall render this glimpse,
Of honey, or give money,
To Peleg… » Said the Queen, loud.

Curriculum Vitae of the poet…

To whom it may concern !

They say I am a poet, a philosopher,
They also call me an inventor, an author,
I heard that I am a worthy abstract painter,
An art collector, and a good photographer…

I used to work directing a large library,
Christian sanctuary for books, old writs, past acts.
I love to keep at my simple home in Paris,
Jewels, gems or seashells, coins, rugs and artifacts…

Then I could say I have been practicing music…

I am a believer in the Might of our Lord,
I pray for salvation to the ones who adored.

And my personal studies have been eclectic,
Through various matters, from the fields, to the sky.
I can run, trek, swim, sail, bike, drive, horse-ride, and ski.

Dedication

To thee Muses of Parnassus,
To thee, Three Dark Norns, in the skies,
Might our Lord bless you, bless us,
Might thee I pray take care of I…

A humble poet, simple man,
Who write here in my solitude,
May I express the gratitude,
That is wise, to you, as I can.

Are we not humans, poor beings ?
In the perspective of our life,
Little measures, short wins, brief strife…

Though you are for sure all - giving,
Thus if you allow me to write,
I will compliment you, albeit…

Goodbye for now !

My name is Timothee, from France,
A man, a friend to the simple…
I have loved some women, by chance,
I have faith in Jesus' angels.

To you esteemed reader, blessing !
I wish all the best for your time,
You have been through these idle rhymes,
Forgive please, their naive writing.

Might our Lord save me, I pray !
I think our lives can be better,
If we work calmly, to progress.

Then I heard, many prophets say,
Paradise would rule all later !
Forever justifying grace…

Timothée Bordenave in Paris, France !
May 2025.

About the Author

Timothée Bordenave

Timothée Bordenave is a French author of fiction, poetry, and essays. He has published many books in France and his literary works have also been published and translated in various other countries… He is also an international visual artist, who held numerous shows of paintings and photographs. He used to work as a director of libraries in Paris, where he still lives today.

www.ingramcontent.com/pod-product-compliance
Lightning Source LLC
LaVergne TN
LVHW041639070526
838199LV00052B/3451